This edition published in 1998 by
Birlinn Limited, Canongate Venture, 5 New Street, Edinburgh EH8 8BH

ISBN 1 874744 63 7

A CIP record of this book is available from the British Library

Typeset by Waverley Typesetters, Galashiels
Printed and bound in Great Britain by Bell & Bain Limited, Glasgow

MIDGES

Midges. The scourge of the west, the terror of the Highlands. In itself chust nothing at all; *meanbh chuileag*, the tiny fly. Wingspan — 1.4 millimetres, but the numbers of them! By the hundred, and the thousand, lying and hatching, and up they rise to bite and suck and torment. One midge bite — nothing. Ten — a mere itch. But by the dozen, and the dozen to the second, flying round your head, biting, drawing . . .

You swat and kill one or two; kill a midge, as they say in Raasay, and a hundred come to the funeral. You swat and flail, clawing at your scalp, cursing. But a cloud of them hangs about your head, fluxing, intangible. They land and walk and puncture. They seek the sweet, sweaty parts of your fizzog — the nostrils, at your hairline, in your brows.

ONE MIDGE NO PROBLEM

TEN A MERE ITCH....

BUT......

OH BRING TO ME A PINT OF BLOOD
AND PUT IT IN A SONSIE TOURIST
THAT I MAY BREED BEFORE I GO.
GERMAN OR SCOTS, I AM NO PURIST.

Only the female midge bites. She bites not to eat, but as part of her reproductive cycle, after she has begun pregnancy. Brave scientists assessed her biting rate in the post-war midge trials — hungry gravid lady midges attack in many dozens, and as many as 2,000 to 3,000 bites an hour were recorded. (John Macleod, *The Herald*, 4 September 1993)

The Highland midge, *Culicoides impunctatus*, is found mainly in areas where annual rainfall exceeds 50 inches, so the west side of Scotland has the greatest reputation for them. In 1990 220 inches fell on Lochaber. Thirty days is long life to a midge but new generations appear through summer. The first-born are males which do not bite, and it is usually June before females go in search of blood-meals. Male midges feed on plant juices. The biting season is only about 10 weeks but so is the tourist season. Midge larvae spend 10 months in a non-feeding state from one year to the next, but then develop from the state of tiny worms to tiny adults in a few days. Up to eighty eggs are produced in a first batch, using energy stored from the non-feeding stage. Mating takes place when the male's antennae detect the high-pitched vibration of the female's wings, triumphant after a blood meal. A second batch of eggs can then be laid. Females

LOCHABER
NO MORE.

NO MIDGIES
MORAG

AYE
DROWNING
IS
PREFERABLE
JEAN

HOUSEWIVES GOSSIP
BESIDE RAIN GAUGE.
LOCHABER 1990

GREAT GRANDMA WAS TERRIBLY
BOTHERED BY MIDGES....

find blood by detecting the carbon dioxide breathed out by humans, horses, cattle and deer. Midge 'bites' are produced when the insect's mouthparts use a scissor-like movement to rasp, not pierce, the outer skin. Hollow, like a hypodermic needle, these then penetrate the tissues under the skin.

The scientist Alison Blackwell assured the author that women are more at risk than men. Not in the author's family they aren't. But people vary in their attractiveness to midges — partly because of being bitten already. No, this is not like innoculation but the reverse. Visitors have an immune system which does not respond to midge bites for a few days. Locals who risk their skin year-in, year-out bringing in the hay are just as likely to be affected as tourists: 'If it is any consolation there are a great many Highlanders who, to their dying day, suffer just as much as the tourist after the first week of a holiday in the area.' (George Hendry, *Midges in Scotland*, 1987)

HISTORY

The Water Poet John Taylor, a favourite at the London court of a Scottish king, James VI and I, decided to experience Macbeth's blasted heath for himself. In Glenesk on a summer day in 1621 the poet found himself in mist, 'wetting me to the skinne, so that my teeth began to dance within my head with cold'. The insects stayed out of the rain. Taylor found an inn, 'sup'd and went to bed, where I had not lain long but I was forced to rise, I was so stung with Irish musketaes, a creature that had 6 legs.' It is hard to imagine 'Irish' — meaning Erse or Gaelic-speaking — midges lying in wait like this. The insects in question were probably mosquitoes indeed.

The Rev. John Morrison was Presbyterian minister of Gairloch, in the Mackenzie country, at a time when most of the clan were Episcopalians. After a long sermon in September 1711, Morrison's congregation at Letterewe stripped the minister of his clerical garb and left him tied to a tree. It was past the worst of the biting season but midge swarms came all the same, and it was late in the evening, as darkness began to cover his nakedness, that a woman took pity and set him free. Morrison fled to Sutherland.

THE REVEREND JOHN MORRISON VOWS TO PREACH SHORTER SERMONS.

Another preacher, Martin Martin of Skye, had a keen eye for flora and fauna — including the least of God's creatures:

The Land, and the Sea that encompasses it, produce many things useful and curious in their kind, several of which have not hitherto been mention'd by the Learned. This may afford the Theorist Subject of Contemplation, since every Plant of the Field, every Fiber of each Plant, and the least Particle of the smallest Insect, carries with it the impress of its Maker.

(*A Description of the Western Islands of Scotland*, 1716)

The Rev. W. Derham was Rector of Upminster; his *Physio-Theology: or a Demonstration of the Being and Attributes of God, from His Works of Creation*, dedicated to the Archbishop of Canterbury in 1713, explained:

For an instance of Insects endowed with a Spear, I shall, for its peculiarity, pitch upon one of the smallest. Among us in Essex they are called Nidiots. *These Gnats are greedy Blood-suckers that have lately befallen near us, in the Parish of Dagenham; where I found them so vexatious that I was glad to get out of these marshes. Yea, I have seen Horses so stung with them that they have had drops of Blood all over their Bodies, where they were wounded by them.*

But *Culex minimus*, as Derham called the creature that lay 'quietly on top of the Water, now and then wagging its tail this way and that', can hardly have been the Highland midge: the closest Essex Man ever came to Caledonia stern and wild was the Dagenham Girl Pipers, a kilted group before the Beatles.

Edmund Burt, a Londoner, built military roads north of Fort William to control the Highlands after the Rising of 1715. Here he is at Fort Augustus:

> *I have but one Thing more to take Notice of in relation to the Spot of which I have been so long speaking, and that is, I have been sometimes vexed with a little Plague (if I may use the Expression), but do not you think I am too grave upon the Subject; there are great Swarms of little Flies which the Natives call* Malhoulakins: Houlak, *they tell me, signifies in the Country Language, a Fly, and* Houlakin *is the Diminutive of that Name. These are so very small, that, separately, they are but just perceptible and that is all; and, being of a blackish colour, when a number of them settle on the skin, they make it look as if it was dirty; there they bore with their little augers into the pores, and change the face from black to red.*
>
> *They are only troublesome (I should say intolerable) in Summer, when there is a profound Calm; for the least Breath of Wind immediately disperses them; and the only Refuge from them is the House, into which I never knew them to enter. Sometimes, when I have been talking to any one, I have (though with the utmost Self-denial) endured their Stings to watch his Face, and see how long they would suffer him to be quiet; but in three or four Seconds, he has slapped his Hand upon his Face, and in great Wrath cursed the little Vermin.*
>
> (*Letters from a Gentleman in the North of Scotland*, 1754)

The keeper of Oxford's Ashmolean Museum, Edward Lhuyd, reached Scotland in 1699 on his tour of Celtic countries. Lhuyd's collection of 'charms for preventing diseases in man or beast' recorded nothing about midges, and the lack of a popular Gaelic name for the midge, beyond tiny fly, casts doubt on it as a native. The bards are silent. The Blind Harper never sang of them at Dunvegan. *Mac Mhaighstir Alasdair* encountered none between Knoydart and Ardnamurchan. In his *Song of Summer* the only insects are *beachach* (bees) and *seilleanach* (wasps) despite perfect conditions for midges — *ciurach, dealtach, trom, blath* (misty, dewy, heavy, warm). Even when the poet calls down biting insects on Eigneig, in Arisaig, and its anti-Jacobite priest, there are no midges: 'And every beast that on me preyed — the wasp, the gadfly and the bee.'

Outsiders became fascinated in the 18th century by *Ossian*, James MacPherson's tales of a legendary Gaelic past. Literary people came north, some already devoted to high lands like the Wordsworths. Enthusiasm for the Highland Tour was a European phenomenon. Visitors kept diaries, many found publishers, but none mentioned midge bites. Thomas Thornton, an early sportsman in the Highlands, pursued a great variety of birds, beasts and fish during the 1780s: 'July 26. Day charming. Went to some lochs . . . Said to be six miles off, but turned out ten. The day was too calm.' Twenty-seven trout were caught to provide a loch-side meal at the end of the day. No biting insects disturbed the sportsman or his ghillies while they ate. Compare this with a modern fisherman's tale.

MIDGES

We pitched camp in the dusk on the bealach *[pass] between Loch Hourn and Loch Quoich beside the tiny* Loch a' Choire Bheithe. *Although the normally boggy hollow was merely moist after the drought, it was still an idiotic choice, harbouring the most feared of Highland predators. As we pitched our tents clouds of midges joyfully attacked the source of fresh blood, making our task a misery. At least I had the foresight to keep my inner tent zipped tight. John tried, very stoically, to fish the lochan but merely served as dessert for the thickening swarms of tiny winged beasts.*

Meanwhile I had built a fire of bogwood on the largest and flattest boulder and sought sanctuary from the midges in the thick drifting smoke. Once John had abandoned his fishing we supped and talked and drank on our smokey boulder and forgot the midges. They had remembered us. As I doused the fire and packed away the food, John tried washing in the burn. The midges regrouped and surrounded him as he tried to get dry, dressed and into his tent. He hardly tarried, but those few moments saw him bitten scarlet and his tent filled with midges. During the rest of the night the threshing of body and limbs and the dejected groans from his tent became increasingly pitiful.

(James McLeod, *The Scotsman*, 29 June 1985)

8

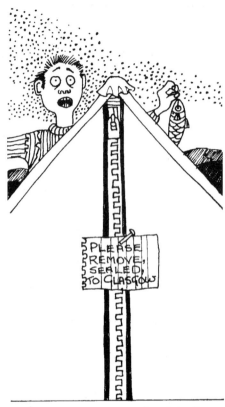

CAMPING AND FISHING
ARE POPULAR
TOURIST PURSUITS

James Hogg, the Ettrick Shepherd, experienced bedbugs in an inn, which shows that journal-writers did not ignore insects:

> *I got the best bed, but it was extremely hard, and the clothes had not the smell of roses. It was also inhabited by a number of little insects common enough in such places, and no sooner had I made a lodgement in their hereditary domains than I was attacked by a thousand strong.*
>
> (*A Journey through the Highlands*, 1804)

Robert Burns, breaking his Highland journey on the notoriously midgy banks of Loch Lomond, found nothing to complain of. He spent a night of festivity in the mansion of a Highland gentleman and used the swarming of tiny creatures to convey a cheerful image of Scottish country dancing: 'The ladies sung Scotch songs like angels, at intervals; then we flew at Bab the Bowster, Tullochgorum, Loch Errol Side, &c, like midges sporting in the mottie sun, or craws prognosticating a storm in a hairst [harvest] day.' (*Tours of the Highlands and Stirlingshire*, 1787)

The midges which Burns knew, dancing in dusty sunlight, were obviously the garden variety (*C. obsoletus*) which scarcely bite. In Lowland Scotland as well as England 'midge' has always meant tiny, with no suggestion of biting. Scripture supports this. In Matthew xxiii, 24, fastidious Pharisees are condemned as 'Blind guides! You strain off a midge and gulp down a camel!' or in the Scots Bible 'clengeand a myge bot suelliand a camele'. The same relaxed attitude was common in the Highlands where, as a proverb had it, 'The cow is only a good deal bigger than the midge.'

MIDGES

The argument that Highland midges were little known in the early 19th century gains support from the silence of Professor John Wilson of Edinburgh University. In an account of a walking tour in the 1820s he wrote 127 pages on 'The Moors' without mentioning them. He did mention ants:

> *Go to a desert and clap your back against a cliff. Do you think yourself alone? What a ninny! Your great clumsy splay feet are bruising to death a batch of beetles. See that spider whom you have widowed, running up and down your elegant leg. Meanwhile your shoulders have crushed a colony of small red ants settled in a moss city beautifully roofed with lichens — and that accounts for the sharp tickling behind your ear, which you keep scratching . . . All the while you are supposing yourself alone! But the whole wilderness — as you choose to call it — is crawling with various life.*
>
> (J. Wilson, *Recreations of Christopher North*, 1865)

Thirty years later Charles Weld provided a striking contrast on a Caithness fishing trip:

> *Talk of solitude on the moors! — why, every square yard contains a population of millions of these little harpies, that pump blood out of you with amazing savageness and insatiability. Where they come from is a puzzle. While you are in motion not one is visible, but when you stop a mist seems to curl about your feet and legs, rising, and at the same time expanding, until you become painfully sensible that the appearance is due to a cloud of gnats. When seven miles from Scourie, I came to the Laxford, a glorious salmon river spanned by a bridge, backed by Ben Stack and framed by rocks, garlanded by fern and birch. A lovely subject for a sketch, but, in my case, unsketchable, for I had no longer sat down than up rose millions of midges, which sent me reeling down the craggy steep, half mad.*
>
> (*Two Months in the Highlands*, 1860)

Timothy Pont's 16th-century map of Edrachillis proclaimed, 'All heir ar black flies in this wood . . . scene souking me[n]'s blood'. Midges or clegs? Three centuries later when army engineers turned to map-making, there was no doubt:

The heat also then being intense above Loch Maree and Gairloch, it was our practice in walking to put our coats and waistcoats into our knapsacks, and thus, with our shirt necks thrown open, and our sleeves tucked up, we were exposed in a peculiar manner to the baneful attacks of those venomous insects. On the occasion referred to we suffered very severely; our arms, necks and faces were covered with scarlet pimples, and we lost several hours' rest at night from the intense itching and pain which they caused. Even at the inns we had frequently to smoke in our bedrooms and over our meals to drive these insects away.

(J. E. Portlock, *Major-General Colby*, 1869)

ENVIRONMENT

The father of the conservation movement in Scotland, Frank Fraser Darling, saw a problem without a solution:

> *Almost everywhere in the Highlands below 2,000 feet there are vast hordes of midges which affect the movements of mammalian life, including man, to a considerable extent. The place of the midge in human ecology is such that a greatly increased tourist industry to the West Highlands could be encouraged if the midge could be controlled. But every square yard of Highland and Island moors has its midges. Little if anything can be done by way of control which would not cause extensive damage to agriculture, forestry, game and freshwater fisheries.'*
> (*The Highlands of Scotland*, 1964)

The French government succeeded in eliminating the mosquito west of Marseille in the 1970s, turning their south-west Mediterranean coastline into another Côte d'Azur. Scotland's tourist industry proclaims that 'One visit is never enough' — but it

12

may be. There is no marketing research to prove that midges deter return visits to the Highlands, despite dark rumours of suppressed evidence in the vaults of the Tourist Board. While monitoring everything from bed nights to bus parties, the question is never put. Perhaps it only applies to those visitors — their accommodation ranging from youth hostels to shooting lodges — who come for the outdoor environment.

Some conservationists would resist the drainage of breeding grounds out of regard for the Highlands as 'unspoiled wilderness'. They are probably unaware of the extent to which that wilderness has been created in modern times. When the Highland Clearances removed people in favour of sheep, in the first half of the 19th century, the landlords appear to have brought about an increase in the midge population. Large tracts were subjected to heather burning to increase sheep pasture. James Hunter argues that the old agricultural system left the new sheep graziers fertile upland pastures which were used for only a few months by cattle. The 'sheep-sick' environment was discussed when lambing percentages fell later, but it was in the 1850s that deterioration of land fertilised by cattle began due to 'purely extractive' sheep farming. (*Northern Scotland*, 1973)

'It is natural, in traversing this gloom of desolation, to inquire whether . . . those hills and moors that afford heath cannot with a little care and labour bear something better? The first thought that occurs is to cover them with trees.' Thus Samuel Johnson — but what kind of trees? High ground has been seeded with conifers this century but there is a difference between natural woodland and forestry plantation. The loss of natural woodland and the rise of forestry estates have combined to provide habitats congenial to midges, with a reduction in the dragonflies and frogs which prey on larvae. Forestry gives shelter from wind and shade from sunlight. Bracken also favours the insects. The Three Curses of Argyll are 'the Bracken, the Midges and the Campbells'. Bracken spreads where arable land is neglected and offers shade.

We will never recover 'the great forest of Caledon', but woodland can return. Sir John Lister-Kaye, who chairs the north-west area (Shetland to Argyll) of Scottish Natural Heritage, suggests that estate owners should give up 15 per cent of their hill units to natural restoration for 25 years. Aware that sheep and deer have 'enormously depleted the natural fertility of the original woodlands', Sir John visualises 'a jigsaw of restoration right across the Highlands and Islands'. Prince Charles agrees: 'The type of sustainable land management ethic advocated by John Lister-Kaye is, I believe, a key part of a more balanced and long-term approach to the management of the fragile Highland ecosystem and the equally fragile human communities which depend upon it.'

In the 17th century climatic change came to the Atlantic edge of Europe. A lowering of sea temperatures brought down Scotland's snow-line by 400 metres, and that greatly reduced the area available for breeding. Cold winters affect the survival of midge larvae and chilly summers the eggs born of blood meals. Long before global warming, temperatures also rose in the early 18th century — hence Burt's 'troublesome' midges.

PRINCE IN THE HEATHER

Charles Edward Stuart made an enforced and extended tour of the Highlands and Islands after the defeat at Culloden in 1746, and was bitten by *C. impunctatus*. In June the no longer Bonny Prince Charlie was in Uist, sheltering under a sail in the heather near Loch Eynort. One of his party wrote of the ordeal, 'We were never a day or night without rain; the Prince was in a terrible condition, his legs & thy's cut all over from the bryers; the mitches or flys wch are terrible in yt contry, devored him, & made him scratch those scars, wch made him appear as if he was cover'd with ulsers.' (A. and H. Tayler, *1745 and After*, 1938) The playwright George Rosie made a link with the Prince's broken-down condition in 1784, when Charles held court in Florence: 'His formerly superb physique is in a state of collapse. He has scurvy sores on his legs which cannot be healed, and cause him constant pain.' (*Carluccio and the Queen of Hearts*, 1992)

'Over the Sea to Skye' seemed the right idea, but midges were not finished with the royal fugitive. John MacDonald of Borrodale was with his Prince in Glenmoriston on 28th July:

> *The evening being very calm and warm, we greatly suffered by mitches, a species of little creatures troublesome and numerous in the highlands; to preserve him from such troublesome guests, we wrapt him head and feet in his plead, and covered him with long heather that naturally grew about a bit of hollow ground where we laid him. After leaving him in that posture, he uttered several heavy sighes and groands. We planted ourselves about the best we could.*
>
> (Bishop Forbes, *The Lyon in Mourning*, 1896)

The Catholic prince was not keen on devotional books, or he might have thought of praying to St Jacobus. This saint brought down clouds of gnats on an army besieging the city of Nisibis and put it to flight. The Jacobites could have used his help against Hanoverian artillery.

NOT EFFECTIVE

CHARLES EDWARD STUART VOWS NEVER TO COME BACK TO SCOTLAND. DIES IN MIDGE FREE ROME

17

Tearlach took to smoking a pipe. Tobacco was a luxury beyond most Gaels, but their lives were permeated by smoke, as visitors noted. John Leyden: 'The huts of the peasants on Mull are most deplorable . . . There is often no other outlet of smoke but at the door, the consequence of which is that the women are more squalid and dirty than the men, and their features more disagreeable.' (*Tour in the Highlands*, 1800)

Robert Southey: 'The smoke is clean, and the smell, to me at least, rather agreeable than otherwise: but it attacks the eyes immediately, and that it injures them is plainly shown by the blear eyes which are here so common among old people.' (*Tour in Scotland*, 1819)

J. E. Bowman, a banker on holiday, took his readers inside a black house:

> *It was formed wholly of turf, the walls not five feet high, and the roof very steep, particularly at one end, where it rose a little higher in a conical shape and ended in a smoke hole . . . I understood from several persons during the tour that the Highlanders are so much attached to their ancient dwellings that they can hardly be persuaded to exchange them for the more comfortable modern cottages. They are certainly much warmer, because the smoke and heated air must fill every cranny before it can escape through the hole in the roof. It is a singular though well ascertained fact that bugs are never found, even in the greatest filth, where peat is used.*
>
> (*The Highlands and Islands*, 1825)

CHUST KIPPERING THE WEANS HAMISH!

GENRE SCENE
SCOTTISH HIGHLANDS

Most visitors regarded the natives as dirty, but in their clothes, hair and skin Gaels were smoked like the herrings they took from sea lochs. Perhaps, Highlanders made brown by turf fires were protected from the midge. Ronald Black, a Gaelic expert at Edinburgh University, thinks so: 'My impression is that midges didn't greatly bother the old Highlanders: while not unwashed, their skin was certainly kippered by peat-reek, as old photographs show.'

Kilts

Ragnall Mac Ille Duibh (to give his Gaelic name) has another explanation for the Highlander's tolerance of midges: 'The traditional plaid was both clothing and bedding, and could be drawn about every part of the body as required. That's why the proscription of Highland dress in 1747 aroused more fury than any legislation before or since.' Earlier, the ironmaster Thomas Rawlinson persuaded his workers to wear the small kilt, or philibeg, while working in a foundry at Invergarry. Cynics believe that this Englishman invented the kilt. It eventually replaced the enveloping philimore when Sir Walter Scott reinvented tartan — through his books, and on the ample frame of George IV on a royal visit to Edinburgh. The monarch's best-dressed friend in youth had been Beau Brummel. In middle age he took the precaution of wearing flesh-coloured tights.

EFFECTIVE

PHILABEG. ALL — ENCOMPASSING MIDGE PROTECTION.

Para Handy, skipper of the puffer *Vital Spark*, has a kilt story concerning 'mudges':

What wass there on the island at the time but a chenuine English towerist, wi' a capital red kilt, and, man! but he wass green! He wass that green, the coos of Colonsay would go mooin' along the road efter him, thinkin' he wass gress. He wass one of them English chentlemen that'll be drinking chinger-beer on aal occasions, even when they're dry, and him bein' English, he had seen next to nothing aal his days till he took the boat from West Loch Tarbet. The first night on the island he went out in his kilt, and came back in half an oor to the inns wi' his legs fair peetiful! There iss nothing that the midges like to see among them better than an English towerist with a kilt: the very top wass eaten off his stockins'.

(Neil Munro, *Tales of Para Handy*, 1931)

It is not true that the redcoat soldiers at Culloden bayoneted kilted opponents who needed a hand free for slapping bare legs. Nor is it accurate to say that midges caused the Highland Fling. But there is no doubt that English workmen were brought to the island of Rum to build a castle for the Lancashire industrialist Sir George Bullough and were required, despite their Accrington origins, to wear his Rum tartan kilt. The midges must have been delighted by this prime English leg. Sir George prevented a strike only by agreeing to pay the men a tobacco allowance of tuppence a week.

ROYALTY

The Sutherland estates were the first to experience clearance of the native population, along with their traditional farming. Queen Victoria paid a visit to Dunrobin Castle in 1872, when vast numbers of sheep and deer had been nibbling for more than half a century: 'The heather is very rich all round here. We got out and went into it . . . drove down again, and before we were out of the lower wood, which is close down upon the sea-shore, we stopped to take our tea and coffee but were half devoured by midges.' (Queen Victoria, *Leaves from Our Life in the Highlands*, 1868) Balmoral was chosen as a royal residence because it was in the drier half of the Highlands, but it also had midges:

OUR DEAR QUEEN
ENJOYING A FLY
DRAG. GLASSALT
SHIEL. 1896

> *'She'll insist on taking you to her "little bothy" at Glassalt Shiel. Make sure you cover up, because the midges there are without exception the most voracious that I have ever come across.' He was right. The only known midge repellents were paraffin oil and tobacco smoke, and Rachel was more than happy to follow her sovereign's stout, black-bonneted example and puff and choke away at one cigarette after another.*
>
> (Reay Tannahill, *In Still and Stormy Waters*, 1992)

The novelist exaggerates. Victoria discouraged smoking at Balmoral but once, when John Brown was not looking, she borrowed a great-grand-daughter's cigarette in an attempt to keep midges at bay.

The *Aberdeen Press and Journal* takes special interest in the royal family when they return to Balmoral each summer:

The infamous Scottish midgie is no respector of persons — as the Princess Royal found to her cost yesterday [18 August 1992]. Every swarm of midgies from miles around seemed keen to join the crowds as the princess started her helicopter-hopping tour of the Highlands at Kyle of Lochalsh. Soon businessmen, councillors and officials were literally itching to be presented to her royal highness. And the temptation to swipe away the insects soon overcame etiquette. But blue blood is no protection against the attentions of the pests. The princess, too, had to resort to the occasional rubbing of the royal cheeks as she spoke with her guests.

This reference to Princess Anne's face recalls an assault on her granny. A minister's wife came to the rescue when the Queen Mother was attacked during Highland Games at the Castle of Mey, her country retreat in Caithness. People noticed the Queen Mother was being bitten when she began waving the tiny insects away from her face. A woman nearby whipped out a midge spray from her handbag and applied it, for some reason, to the royal legs.

24

NATURE

Nowadays nobody believes that midges should be attacked with chemical weapons. We have all become aware of how pesticides enter the food chain, threatening various species including ourselves. Do midges do any good, environmentally speaking? On the Russian steppes midges and other blackflies may save the fragile tundra by keeping grazing animals on the move. In Scotland, the grazing patterns of red deer are partly controlled by the midges: 'In summer the severe attacks force the deer up to the higher and more windswept hills.' (Hendry, *Midges in Scotland*) Perhaps more birds in the Highlands would help. When a record number of pied flycatchers was reported in the Inversnaid reserve at Loch Lomond, an RSPB spokesman told the *Glasgow Evening Times*: 'With the swarms of midges around at the moment, which flycatchers eat, the more "pied flies" the better!

BITTEN TO DEATH 1898

The news of a parasitic red mite, small enough for four to live off a single midge and introduced illicitly from Africa by entomologist Eugen Hayek, sounded like a spoof, in a *Private Eye* piece by 'Old Muckspreader'. In November 1992 Lord Fraser of Carmyllie, Minister of State for the Scottish Office, told the Upper House: 'The Red Mite is proving a mite elusive . . . We are not actually sure it exists.' In the following May, however, Britain's traditional landowners were told by a 'red-faced' Lord Fraser that research into its habits was being conducted on behalf of the Natural History Museum. Lord Campbell of Croy saw this as a victory. 'I'm delighted there are people concerned about these beasties,' he told a mirthful House to cries of 'What about the Blandford Fly?'

Anne Baker was funded by the British Entomological Society and spent the summer of 1993 in Skye collecting midges. Only 2 per cent of her sample were weakened by red mites, and 'experts believed that it was not in the interest of the parasite mite to weaken the host midge to the point of death'. This seems a mite obvious to the non-expert. Healthy midges achieve a grand old age of thirty days, with those carrying the dreaded red mite cut down in their twenties. Chronic illness in one midge out of fifty seems a very small step for man.

Science came together with archaeology when it was reported in 1993 that midges and their much-publicised parasites had been in the Highlands since the dawn of time. The programme *Tomorrow's World* announced that a midge fossil had been found in resin, with a mite still attached to it, from 70 million years ago. Lord Fraser saw this as bad news: 'If over that extended period the mite has been unable to bring to an end the primitive midge, it is unlikely within your Lordships' lifetime to achieve any success against the ferocious Highland midge.' But the fossil offers hope that the analysis techniques of archaeology, which have yielded information on insects larger than midges, may come up with evidence about change over the centuries. The answer lies in the the peat bog. Dr Nick Dickson of Edinburgh University denied that he had found midges preserved in a prehistoric crannog or lake-dwelling in Loch Tay. It should soon be possible to identify a range of insects, however, from before the time of Agricola's bare-legged legionnaries.

Linked with red mites, at least in the House of Lords, are bats. Lord Fraser admitted that the natterer's bat sounded 'something like a refugee from a mother-in-law joke', but was able to reveal that it did exist, favouring larger insects while accepting midges too. The pipistrelle bat, however, is said to be able to eat a thousand midges a night, or twice its own weight. In the absence of belfries, bats need more dwelling houses and byres, for roof space, than the Highlands have seen since the Clearances. Is this part of the reason, along with peat smoke, why Gaels were not bothered by midges near home?

SCIENCE

After the last war when the government was considering what might be done, Dr Douglas Kettle of Glasgow University studied the midge's breeding habits near Luss on the banks of Loch Lomond. Other samples were gathered from a 'moorland site' near Glasgow — Drumchapel. Kettle's main interest was in larvae which could be studied out of the biting season. Most were found near the surface of wet soil in bogs, and it was easy enough to bring back samples to the lab and separate out worms — never to fly — with sieves and concentrated magnesium sulphate. '*Culicoides* larvae were readily recognised by their active lashing swimming movements.'

Today animal rights activists would be out with placards: 'Due to the exhaustion of the food supply the larvae failed to grow, although they often survived for long periods.' The phrase 'larval preservation' meant being killed by the aptly named Dr Kettle: 'Living larvae, dropped into hot water were preserved in 70 per cent alcohol.' Later Kettle had very limited success in his attempts to eradicate larvae and midges on their home ground by chemical means. (*Bulletin of Entomological Research*, 1952)

More recently scientists have been going on summer safaris led by Alison Blackwell of Dundee University. Even in winter Alison's arms showed the scars until a protective outfit was devised to make field-workers look like beekeepers. Results are promising:

MIDGES

Scientists working in Argyllshire believe they have discovered the perfect midge bait, a chemical call sign emitted by the insects which alerts others to the prospect of a good meal . . . The researchers believe a synthetic version of the chemical, known as a recruiting pheromone, could be used to lure Culicoides Impunctatus Goetghbuer *into traps by the million.*

(Sunday Times, 13 June 1993)

There were two study sites: Ormsary, Argyllshire, and Kinlochewe in Wester Ross. Searches for swarms were made around dawn and during the 3 to 4 hours before dusk. About a third of the swarms were netted completely and numbers counted.

Precise data emerged for the first time. The electron microscope was used on freeze-dried midges, painted gold. Females turn out to have three times as many olfactory sensilla as tactile hairs on their antennae, reflecting their dependence on smell for finding blood meals. Swarms ranged from single figures to an uncountable one of 3–4,000 midges. The commonest shape was oval and up to 2 metres wide. Swarms were videoed to examine flight paths, traced at 40-millisecond intervals from a colour monitor:

START

THE DANCE OF THE MIDGE.
REPLICATED IN SCOTTISH
COUNTRY DANCING SINCE
MORE THAN TWO WERE
GATHERED TOGETHER IN
THE NAME OF FUN AND
TORTURE.

Each midge flew with a fast zigzagging movement, falling to the bottom of the swarm, circling back up again, pausing briefly and falling again — all in about one second. Midges faced upwind. Downwind drift was recorded, and in gusts of wind swarms would be blown away. Light levels were the primary stimulus for swarm formation. Most swarms occurred one or two hours before sunset in low light, with swarm numbers increasing in still, humid conditions. In ideal climatic conditions C. impunctatus swarms were observed for almost an hour.
(*Ecological Entomology*, 1992)

The tendency of midges to emerge before dusk in conditions of low wind was confirmed by observing insects normally too small for the tracking and trapping techniques of entomology.

Another scientist admitted ignorance: 'The fine details of the mating process are not known, because of the inherent problem of trying to monitor the goings-on of a couple of busy insects only two millimetres long.' (Hendry, *Midges in Scotland*) Thanks to Alison Blackwell, the secrets are out:

PASSING VIRGIN
MIDGE STRUTS HER
STUFF

For males to wait in the vegetation for emerging females may, at times, be sufficient to effect mating. Males would then expend less energy than for swarming and would be sure to mate with young, virgin females which would be maximally receptive. Swarming helps mating. Pairs presumably form within the swarms and complete mating on the ground or a nearby surface. A total of thirty-six copulating C. impunctatus pairs were observed on warm still evenings. Pairs were never seen actually forming, and therefore the copulation times recorded are shorter than the mating times. Some pairs separated almost immediately. Most copulation periods were one to three minutes, although one pair remained united for eighteen minutes.

(*Ecological Entomology*, 1992)

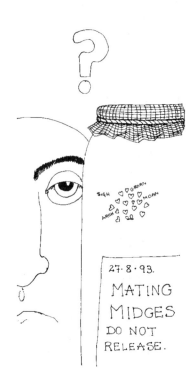

27·8·93.
MATING
MIDGES
DO NOT
RELEASE.

PLACES

'Is it the midges of Skye that are most ferocious? Or the beasties of Achnashellach? Are they more numerous in Glenelg, the bites more painful by Strontian? Midges seem less active in the Outer Isles, where still nights are infrequent — but when they come they bite — and how.' Thus John MacLeod from the Outer Isles, raising a question for anyone planning a holiday route.

Hamish Henderson has spent much of his life roaming the country in search of tinkers — travelling people — or anyone who remembers an old song or story for the School of Scottish Studies in Edinburgh. His own midge memories go back to childhood:

Roaming around the Perthshire Highlands on a push-bike when I was a kid, it always seemed to me that these areas were less midge-infested than areas north and west of the Great Glen. I remember pitching a bivvy at Strome Ferry on a spot which turned out to be their GHQ; some of them got inside the bivvy, and in ten minutes I was nearly bitten to death. These was nothing for it but to abandon the position. This really is an important question from the 'courtesy to tourists' point of view. Visitors to Scotland are entitled to information about the real danger-zones so that they can come prepared — or at any rate forewarned.

(*The Scotsman*, 4 September 1985)

33

He is right: visitors could and should be given advice about places to avoid, summer by summer, apart from the horror stories of other travellers. We are familiar with ski reports: why not midge reports?

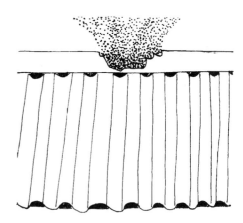

'The Congo's no to be compared wi' the West of Scotland when ye come to insects,' said Para Handy.

'There's places here that's chust deplorable whenever the weather's the least bit warm. Look at Tighnabruaich! — they're that bad there, they'll bite their way through corrugated iron roofs to get at ye! Take Clynder, again, or any other place in the Gareloch, and ye'll see the old ones leadin' roon the young ones, learnin' them the proper grips. There iss a special kind of mudge in Dervaig, in the Isle of Mull, that hass aal the points o' a Poltolloch terrier, even to the black nose and the cocked lugs, and sits up and barks at you.'

'Oh, criftens!' whimpered Sunny Jim, in agony, dabbing his face incessantly with what looked suspiciously like a dish-cloth; 'I've see'd

midges afore this, but they never had spurs on their feet before. Yah-h-h! I wish I was back in Gleska! They can say what they like aboot the Clyde, but anywhere above Bowlin' I'll guarantee ye'll no be eaten alive. If they found a midge in Gleska, they would put it in the Kelvingrove Museum.'

(*Para Handy*)

Regional news came from a poll of workers on twenty-two forestry estate in 1988. 'No effect beyond discomfort' was reported to George Hendry and Gunnar Godwin by the axemen of Loch Tummel and Loch Tay, in contrast to 'Re-scheduled work necessary, operations curtailed or abandoned for several periods in the season' in the wetter, more westerly areas of Kintyre, Lochaber and Wester Ross. Ardgartan, Loch Awe and Fort Augustus fell into the 'rarely serious' category, although conditions were 'often uncomfortable'. More than half of the nationally-owned forests are in the high rainfall west.

The worst forestry tasks for midge attacks are those requiring both hands like draining, planting, weeding, fencing and tree-felling, i.e., most of them: 'The use of helmets and visors also appears to attract midges, possibly from the odour of sweat from poorly ventilated headwear. Although exhaust fumes from chain-saws may deter attacks, at least temporarily, vivid accounts of resumed assaults during re-fueling were provided by several respondents.' All that and the threat of privatisation in a rural industry which increasingly recruits seasonal workers — guess which season. Forestry workers are least troubled during chemical spraying and ploughing — the latter providing 'a protective cab as well as mobility'.

(*Scottish Forestry*, 1988

If Kintyre is bad for forestry workers, the story of 'a Highland home in Cantyre' offered a warning to artists as well:

> *We are exceedingly fortunate in being able to sit here in perfect peace and enjoyment, without being irritated beyond endurance by the bloodthirsty attacks of swarms of midges and gnats. Thus my little illustration of one of the 'pleasures' attendant upon sketching in the Highlands truly depicts a very common occurrence, and one which, while it drives artists to the verge of frenzy, also compels them to adopt mosquito-curtain veils and other extraordinary head-gear, partially protected by which shrouding they may paint under difficulties.*
>
> *One of Mr Leech's inimitable sketches in 'Punch' will doubtless be called to mind, where two artists in the Highlands are thus represented with their heads wonderfully done up in gnat-defiers, in which are glazed eyelet-holes and a mouth piece, through which a sanatory [sic] pipe may be smoked.*
>
> (Cuthbert Bede, *Glencreggan*, 1861)

REMEDIES

NO MIIG WITH MUGWORT

The word 'midge' derives from the Old Norse *muggia* (*mygg* to the Swedes) so it is no surprise that the oldest folk remedy is mugwort (*Artemisia vulgaris*) or midge-plant. In the 16th century it was recommended against insects of all sorts, either as a lotion or burnt in a fire. Over the years many repellents have been tried. If you go down in the woods and stop for a picnic lunch, forest lore says that a cedar tree will provide the best shelter from midges because of the thuja which is found in both red and white species. King Solomon favoured the Lebanon variety and was never bitten by midges in the temple — or anywhere else.

A mixture of 1 part oil of lavender and 20 parts elderflower water was said by *Home Gardening* (May 1928) to be 'very efficacious', one application lasting a whole evening. Far from the suburbs, J. G. Myers, the explorer, favoured oil of pennyroyal (a

EARLY NORWEGIAN ANTI MIDGE HELMET.

species of mint) against mosquitoes. Another remedy is based on 1 oz oil of cassia (extracted from cinnamon bark) with 2 oz camphorated oil — not to be rubbed on the chest in this summertime quest for health and safety. All this is mixed with 3 oz lanoline (the fatty basis of ointments extracted from sheep's wool — though sheep suffer plenty from midges) and 'paraffin wax to stiffen' — for English tourists to apply to the upper lip.

Some time ago *Canadian Entomologist* prescribed 1 part oil of thyme, 2 parts concentrated extract of pyrethrum flowers (Pellitory of Spain, with pungent root) in 2 parts mineral oil and 5 parts castor oil. Oil of white birch (easy to obtain at the lake while birch bark canoe-making) was quite effective — provided Canadian entomologists' wives could stand the smell.

Australians rely on a can of beer. Once the contents have been disposed of in the normal way it is half-filled with vegetable oil, together with a quarter cup of antiseptic and topped up with water — salt water, since this recipe comes from the deep sea fishermen of Queensland. Shark bites are another problem. Application is typically Aussie: shake the can, splash it on — no worries.

Lemon juice has always had supporters, particularly in the combination 1 oz citronella with 4 oz petrol 'as least injurious to the skin', but it turns forestry workers yellow. Green is the environmental colour. *Mosi-guard Natural* is marketed as an alternative to repellents based on DEET (diethyltoluamide) which is dangerous in the bloodstream, especially to children. The natural version of *Mosi-guard*, successfully trialled against African mosquitoes, is mainly eucalyptus oil. In summer 1994 the trial was extended to female zoology students who exposed Mosi-guarded arms in Scotland alongside unguarded 'controls' —they had to show great self-control. There was a rota among the three of them. Up to 187 bites were recorded per exposed arm (in 10 minutes) compared with six on the treated arm. As a distraction, and if possible before the full midge treatment of blood out, saliva in, the students used plastic tubing to suck insects off the skin. They then blew midges into a jar of alcohol for counting, with considerable relish, later.

The consumer magazine *Which* has applied its 'more blobs the better' to 400 brands of insect repellent, on sale as Lotions, Sprays, Sticks and Wipes. Lotions come cheap — best buys *Combat*, *Mijex*, *Mosi-guard*, *Nat-rapel*, *Repel Sportsman* and *Shoo*. Sprays are easy to use — *Mosi-guard* (again) and *Z-Stop* the winners here. *Autan* and *Wild-Life* are the best stick repellents, but no wipe received the *Which* seal of approval since none lasts as long as the average early evening midge attack — enough to dash from car to B&B, though. Smoking insect coils get some support, ultraviolet lamps hardly any. Greatest scorn is reserved for buzzing gadgets meant to mimic amorous male midges: 'Don't buy them — they do not work.'

THE STRICTLY NON-SMOKING McPHEES TRAVELLED THE HIGHLANDS EXISTING ON BOILED HAM AND VENISON PATÉ', PURCHASED IN TESCOS

ESSO BLUE

The journalist Ruth Wishart went to an unlikely factory on the shores of Loch Long to meet the man who invented *Shoo*: 'Paton Cumming's shed has clearly seen better days from a strictly aesthetic point of view. But it has rarely been busier.' His uncle was involved in developing what became DEET for short-trousered soldiers in North Africa and the Far East. By then Imperial Chemical Industries owned the formula, but 'ICI this is not'. Inside, Alan and Jessie are packing ever-growing supplies of *Shoo*, which comes in bottles and wipes. Christened some eight years ago by Paton's grand-daughter, it has already found favour with the Forestry Commission, British Airways, British Telecom, and the lesser spotted gardeners of West and Central Scotland.' (*The Scotsman*, 6 July 1993)

The Hebridean John Macleod emphasises the importance of keeping two old remedies apart: 'Highland tinkers used to swear by neckties soaked in paraffin — 100 per cent effective in most civilized society. I myself used to rely on the fumes of Capstan Full Strength cigarettes, which did for midges what the doctors said they did for your lungs. I stayed a safe distance from tinkers, and their scarves, while indulging.' This prompts memories of the *Vital Spark*:

'I promised I would go up and see Macrae the nicht,' said Macphail. 'But it's no' safe to go up on that quay. This is yin o' the times I wish I was a smoker; that tobacco o' yours, Dougie, would shairly fricht awe' the midges.'

'Not wan bit of it!' said Dougie peevishly, rubbing the back of his neck, on which his tormentors were thickly clustered. 'I'm beginning to think mysel' they're partial to tobacco; it maybe stimulates the appetite. My! Aren't they the brutes! Look at them on Jim!' With a howl of anguish Sunny Jim dashed down the fo'c'stle hatch, the back of his coat pulled over his ears. 'Is there naethin' at a' a chap could dae to his face to keep them aff?' asked the engineer, still solicitous about his promised visit to Macrae.

'Some people'll be sayin' paraffine-oil iss a good thing,' suggested the Captain. But that's only for Ro'sa' mudges; I'm thinkin' the Arrochar mudges would maybe consider paraffine a trate. And I've heard o' others, tryin' whusky — I mean rubbed on ootside. I never had enough to experiment wi't mysel'.'

(Para Handy)

Stirling is the gateway to the Highlands and the obvious place for an annual Midgie Festival Competition: 'Retell your worst experiences with the pernicious Scottish midgy and other man-eating insects in cartoons or humorous tales or verse.' The organiser Eric Allison receives a bulging postbag every year from tourists who have banged the gete behind them, relieved to be back in the Lowlands. Awful puns set the tone of his book.

MIDGES

The cover shows a midge consulting manuals like *Midgesummer Night's Dream* and *Charge of the Bite Brigade*. One tale, perfectly true, begins: 'Why you might ask, were my husband and I, with Siamese Cat on a lead, wandering around the streets of a Scottish town in our pyjamas at four o'clock in the morning?' Best poem? 'They flew oot o' Hell's open windae!' just shades it from 'Let us Spray'. (*The Flight of the Midgie*, 1990)

One remedy reminds us that some people are luckier than others, but biochemistry can help:

> *Since we made our home near Inverness twelve years ago my husband was very seldom bitten but I had only to step outside the door to be attacked by voracious swarms. However after several very 'irritating' season I read a letter in a Sunday paper in which the writer said he couldn't understand what all the fuss was about. He took a strong Vitamin C tablet —200 or 250 mg — before going out (and perhaps another later on if necessary) and he never got bitten by midgies. I tried this and found that, for me, it works splendidly.*
>
> (*The Scotsman*, 3 September 1985)

FINALLY

Of all the insects that have raised bumps and itchy spots on me and drawn blood from my cringing skin, I suppose the Highland midge has caused me the greatest melancholy. I can remember standing on a windless Celtic summer evening watching the hidden sun ring black Mull in a lake of fire. It was a time of prose inspiration and poetic derivation, lofty thoughts about man's place in the universe, and a hush like a benison, all ruined by the fact that local midges were working overtime and making me feel that hundreds of tiny hypodermic needles were being plunged into my face.

Like most people, I have tried a witch's brew of creams and other repellents to make midges, if not curl up and die, at least pause in their tracks. All to no avail. Ancients, wise in the ways of midges, told me that smoke from a pipe tobacco called Navy Cut plug was effective in thwarting them temporarily — rather like a destroyer making smoke for protective purposes — but that fag smokers just suffered. That was not strictly true. Once I smoked black Burmese cheroots and had crafty drags at Balkan cigarettes,

TOBACCO MAY SERIOUSLY DAMAGE MIDGES.

both of which gave out smoke redolent of Eastern bazaars, seraglio nights and a faint whiff of lodging house cat. The midges seemed stunned by the effects of passive smoking and one sensed that they were suddenly coughing and wiping their eyes. After a pause of about 20 minutes, though, they seemed to be getting used to the scent, perhaps even inhaling it with enjoyment, and then having a quiet drink off you as a chaser.

(Albert Morris, *The Scotsman*)

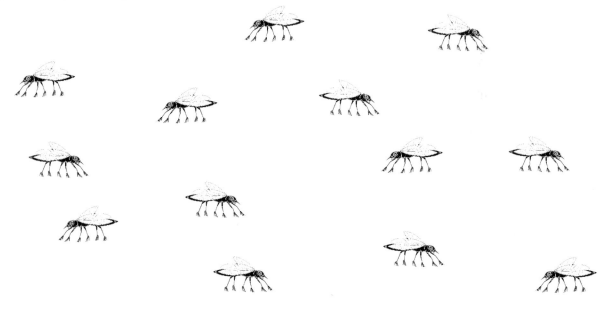